Scottish Slimmers

soup

contents

Key to recipes

SERVES
two

000

0 0

Checks

Calories

Fat
grams

All values given in the recipes are for calories, Checks and grams of fat (in that order), excluding No-Check foods, and are **per serving** unless stated otherwise.

no-check soup

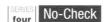
SERVES four | No-Check

carrot & coriander soup

- **1 onion, chopped**
- **1 clove garlic, crushed**
- **350g/12 oz carrots, sliced**
- **900 ml/1½ pints chicken or vegetable stock**
- **2 tbsp chopped coriander**
- **sprigs of coriander to garnish**

1 Place all ingredients into a saucepan. Bring to the boil, cover, reduce heat and simmer about 20 minutes.

2 Allow to cool slightly then liquidise until smooth.

3 If necessary, re-heat gently and serve garnished with a sprig of coriander.

cauliflower & broccoli soup

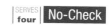

- 250g/9 oz fresh or frozen cauliflower florets
- 250g/9 oz fresh or frozen broccoli florets
- 1 onion, chopped
- 900 ml/1½ pints chicken or vegetable stock
- grated nutmeg to garnish

1 Place all vegetables in a large saucepan and add the stock.

2 Bring to the boil, cover, reduce heat and simmer about 20 minutes.

3 Allow to cool slightly then liquidise to desired texture.

4 Serve garnished with a grating of nutmeg.

SERVES four	No-Check

french onion soup

450g/1 lb onions, sliced
900 ml/1½ pints beef stock
pepper

1 Place onion slices in a large saucepan with 2 tbsp water. Cover and cook gently 10 minutes.

2 Stir onion, add another 2 tbsp water, cover and continue to cook gently a further 10 minutes.

3 Remove lid, turn up heat and stir-fry until water has evaporated and onions turn golden brown.

4 Stir in beef stock and warm through. Season with pepper.

variation...

Garnish with 1 tbsp finely grated half-fat mature cheddar (approx. 5g) and add 15 calories, ½ Check, 1g fat.

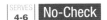

SERVES 4-6 | **No-Check**

leek & carrot soup

- **300g/10 oz small young carrots**
- **300g/10 oz washed and trimmed leeks**
- **900ml/1½ pints water**
- **2 Oxo vegetable cubes**

1 Peel and slice the carrots thinly. Slice the washed and trimmed leeks thinly. Put carrots and leeks into a large saucepan.

2 Add water and crumble in Oxo cubes. Stir well. Cover and bring to the boil.

3 Turn down heat and simmer covered for about 10-15 minutes, stirring occasionally.

tip:

To crumble Oxo cubes, open out the four folded points and side flaps. Use your fist to gently crush the contents of the cube and form a little pillow. Tear off end and shake out contents.

tomato, green bean & balsamic vinegar soup

SERVES four | **No-Check**

- 600ml/1 pint vegetable stock
- 115g/4 oz frozen sliced green beans
- 400g can chopped tomatoes
- 1 tbsp balsamic vinegar
- 1 tsp granulated sweetener
- black pepper

1 Bring the vegetable stock to the boil in a large saucepan. Whilst frozen, snap in half any green beans that look particularly long. Add the frozen beans to the stock and return to the boil. Reduce heat and simmer 5 minutes.

2 Stir in the chopped tomatoes and balsamic vinegar. Bring back to a simmer and continue to cook 5 minutes.

3 Stir in the granulated sweetener and season lightly with black pepper.

spicy
soup

SERVES		
four	75	**3** ②

tom yum

- 2 tsp Thai red curry paste
- 225g/8oz chicken breast fillets, finely chopped
- 115g/4oz shitake or chestnut mushrooms, sliced
- 900 ml/1½ pints hot chicken stock
- 1 stick lemon grass, finely chopped
- 2.5cm/1 inch piece fresh ginger, peeled and grated
- 3 tsp tamarind paste
- 3 fresh or dried lime leaves (optional)
- juice of 1 lime
- torn coriander leaves to garnish

1 Heat the curry paste in a large saucepan and cook gently for 1 minute over medium heat. Add the chicken and mushrooms and stir until well coated with the paste.

2 Pour in the hot chicken stock and stir in the lemon grass, ginger, tamarind and lime leaves.

3 Bring the soup to the boil, reduce heat to a bare simmer and cook gently a further 5 minutes.

4 Stir in the lime juice and spring onions and serve garnished with torn coriander.

curried butternut squash soup

SERVES 4-6 | No-Check

- **1 medium butternut squash, peeled and cubed**
- **2 medium onions, chopped**
- **2 sticks celery, sliced**
- **2 cloves garlic, crushed**
- **1 tbsp curry powder, or to taste**
- **1 Oxo chicken or vegetable cube**

1 Place all ingredients in a large saucepan and cover with water. Bring to the boil, then cover and simmer until vegetables are soft, stirring now and again.

2 Allow to cool a little then liquidise until smooth, adding extra water if necessary.

3 This soup is best left for a few hours for flavours to develop. Re-heat gently before serving.

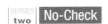

SERVES **two** | **No-Check**

hot & sour soup

- **6 mushrooms, sliced**
- **4 spring onions, trimmed and sliced**
- **½ -1 red or green chilli, de-seeded and finely sliced**
- **2 tbsp light soy sauce**
- **1 dspn vinegar**
- **1 tbsp tomato purée**
- **750ml/1¼ pints water**
- **150g/ 5oz beansprouts**

1 Place all ingredients except beansprouts into a saucepan. Bring to the boil, turn down heat and simmer 5 minutes.

2 Add beansprouts and simmer 1 minute more.

variation...

Add 115g/4oz firm tofu cut into 1 cm/½ inch cubes at the beginning of cooking for an even more nutritious soup meal. Count 30 cals, 1 Check, 1.5g fat per serving.

SERVES
four **No-Check**

muligatawny

200g/7oz onions, sliced
200g/7oz carrots, sliced
150ml/¼ pint water
1 tbsp hot Madras curry powder (or to taste)
2 x 400g cans tomatoes
2 Bovril beef cubes

1 Place carrots and onions into a saucepan with the water. Bring to the boil, cover, reduce heat and simmer 10 minutes.

2 Remove lid and stir in the curry powder. Add tomatoes, breaking them up, and crumble in Bovril cubes. Stir well, cover and simmer 15 minutes.

3 Allow to cool a little and either liquidise all the soup, or liquidise half the soup and mix with remaining half. If too thick, stir in additional water.

4 Re-heat gently before serving.

spicy bean & pepper soup

SERVES six 50 2 0

- **1 medium onion, chopped**
- **1 clove garlic, crushed**
- **115g/4oz frozen sliced mixed peppers**
- **2 x 400g cans chopped tomatoes**
- **1 tsp chilli or hot chilli powder, or to taste**
- **½ tsp cumin**
- **1 Oxo beef or vegetable or Bovril cube**
- **400g approx. can of beans (e.g. kidney beans, cannellini beans, borlotti beans, black-eyed beans)**
- **600ml/1 pint water**

1 Place the onions, garlic and peppers into a large saucepan and stir-fry until softened and starting to colour.

2 Stir in tomatoes, chilli powder, cumin and stock cube.

3 Rinse and drain the beans and add to the pan together with the water. Bring to a gentle simmer, cover and cook about 20 minutes for flavours to develop. Check and stir now and again.

substantial soup

SERVES four | 140 6 2

manhattan fish chowder

spray oil
1 large onion, finely chopped
1 red pepper, de-seeded and chopped
60g/2oz well trimmed, smoked lean back bacon, diced
250g/9oz potatoes, peeled and diced
600ml/1 pint fish or vegetable stock
400g can chopped tomatoes
few sprigs fresh thyme
1 bay leaf
300g can baby clams in brine, drained
175g/6oz skinned fillet cod or haddock, cubed
salt and black pepper
dash of Tabasco
small sprigs of thyme or chopped flat leaf parsley to garnish

1 Spray a large saucepan with oil and cook the onion, red pepper and bacon over medium heat until the vegetables are softened and the bacon lightly browned.

2 Add the potatoes and continue cooking 2-3 minutes stirring gently.

3 Add the stock, tomatoes and herbs and bring to the boil. Reduce heat and simmer about 10 minutes then add the clams and cod or haddock. Cook gently for a further 10-15 minutes.

4 Season to taste with salt, pepper and Tabasco and serve garnished with small sprigs of thyme or flat leaf parsley.

lentil &
bacon pot

- 450ml/¾ pint water
- 100g/3½ oz puy (small green) lentils
- 1 onion, chopped
- 2 medium carrots, diced
- 2 sticks celery, sliced
- 1 clove garlic, chopped
- 600ml/1 pint hot water
- 250g/9 oz potatoes
- 4 rashers, well trimmed, lean back bacon, chopped
- 1 Oxo chicken cube
- salt and pepper
- 1 tbsp chopped fresh parsley

1 Bring cold water to the boil in a large saucepan. Add lentils and boil 10 minutes. Add onions, carrots, celery, garlic and hot water. Bring back to the boil, then turn down heat, cover and simmer 30 minutes.

2 Peel potatoes and cut into 1 cm/½ inch cubes. Add to the pan together with the bacon. Cover and simmer a further 15 minutes, or until lentils and potatoes are cooked.

3 Crumble and stir in chicken cube and season to taste. Sprinkle with fresh parsley before serving.

SERVES | four | 145 6 5

chickpea soup with houmous

spray oil
1 large onion, chopped
2 cloves garlic, crushed
1 tsp coriander seeds, crushed
2 x 400g cans chickpeas, drained
900ml/1½ pints boiling vegetable stock
1 tsp ground turmeric
½ tsp ground cumin
salt and black pepper
4 tsp 0% fat greek yoghurt
4 tsp reduced-fat houmous
pinch of chilli powder (optional)
fresh coriander to garnish

1 Spray a large saucepan with oil and sauté the onion and garlic until softened. Add the coriander seeds and cook 1 minute.

2 Add most of the chickpeas, reserving a few for the garnish. Pour in the boiling stock and bring to the boil. Reduce the heat to a simmer and stir in the turmeric and cumin. Cook gently, uncovered, for 15-20 minutes.

3 Allow to cool slightly then liquidise the soup in batches until thick and smooth. Return to a clean pan and heat through gently, seasoning to taste.

4 Serve the soup in bowls. Swirl in the yoghurt and houmous and sprinkle with chilli powder (if using) and the reserved chickpeas. Garnish with fresh coriander.

SERVES | **65** **2.5** ②
six

minestrone

1 medium onion, chopped
1 clove garlic, crushed
1 medium carrot, diced
1 small turnip, diced
1 medium leek, trimmed, washed and sliced
1 celery stalk, sliced
1200ml/2 pints chicken or vegetable stock
2 tbsp tomato purée
60g/2oz small soup pasta or broken spaghetti
115g/4oz savoy cabbage, finely shredded
115g/4oz frozen sliced green beans
salt and black pepper
6 level dspn grated parmesan cheese

1 Place the onions, garlic, carrot, turnip, leek and celery in a large saucepan. Stir in the stock and tomato purée. Bring to the boil, reduce heat, cover and simmer 30 minutes or until vegetables are tender. Check and stir now and again.

2 Add the soup pasta, cabbage and beans. Return to the boil, reduce heat, cover and simmer a further 15 minutes. Season to taste.

3 Serve each bowl sprinkled with 1 dspn grated parmesan cheese.

celery hearts & butterbean soup

SERVES **six** | 75 **3** 0

- 2 celery hearts, chopped
- 400g can chopped tomatoes
- 300g/10oz potatoes, peeled and cubed
- 1200ml/2 pints chicken or vegetable stock
- salt and pepper
- 300g can butterbeans, drained and rinsed

1 Place the celery hearts, tomatoes and potatoes in a large saucepan and add the stock. Bring to the boil, reduce the heat, cover and simmer 30 minutes. Check and stir now and again.

2 Allow to cool slightly then liquidise three-quarters of the soup. Return to the pan and season to taste.

3 Add the butterbeans, re-heat gently and serve.

light &
fresh
soup

SERVES four 30 **1** 0

watercress soup

175g/6 oz watercress
1 medium onion, chopped
750ml/1¼ pints chicken or vegetable stock
salt and pepper
4 level tbsp skimmed milk powder
2 level tsp cornflour
150ml/¼ pint chicken or vegetable stock
6 level tbsp fat-free natural fromage frais

1 Wash watercress and discard stalks if tough.

2 Boil chopped onions in the larger amount of stock for 10 minutes. Add salt and pepper to taste. Add watercress and simmer for another 10 minutes.

3 Allow to cool slightly then liquidise.

4 Blend milk powder and cornflour with the smaller amount of stock. Add to the soup then return to the pan. Bring to the boil, stirring continuously, until soup thickens. Simmer 2-3 minutes.

5 Serve each bowl with a swirl of fromage frais, which can be stirred into the soup.

salad soup

SERVES **two** | 50 | **2** **0**

- **150ml/¼ pint water**
- **1 Oxo vegetable cube**
- **150g/5oz iceberg lettuce**
- **85g/3oz cucumber**
- **3 spring onions**
- **300ml/½ pint skimmed milk**
- **black pepper**

1 Put water into a medium saucepan, stir in crumbled cube and bring to the boil.

2 Roughly chop the vegetables, add to the pan and simmer 2 minutes.

3 Put milk into a blender, add contents of the saucepan and liquidise until smooth. Re-heat gently and season with black pepper.

4 Either serve warm, or allow to cool, refrigerate and serve chilled.

SERVES two | 100 **4** 1

prawn & mushroom soup

- 85g/3oz mushrooms, sliced
- 200ml/ ⅓ pint chicken stock
- 2 tbsp white wine
- 300ml/½ pint skimmed milk
- 85g/3oz cooked prawns, defrosted if frozen
- black pepper
- 1 tsp finely chopped parsley

1 Place the mushrooms, stock and wine in a medium saucepan. Bring to a simmer and cook 3 minutes.

2 Stir in milk and prawns and heat through gently. Do not allow to boil. Season to taste with black pepper.

3 Serve garnished with chopped parsley.

apple & courgette soup

SERVES | four | 95

- spray oil
- 1 large onion, chopped
- 1 cooking apple, peeled, cored and chopped
- 1 dspn curry powder
- 750ml/1¼ pints chicken or vegetable stock
- 60g/2oz long grain rice
- 2 medium courgettes, chopped
- 300ml/½ pint semi-skimmed milk

1 Spray a large saucepan with oil. Sauté onion and apple until soft. Sprinkle with curry powder and cook, stirring, for a few seconds.

2 Pour in stock and bring to the boil. Add rice and courgettes, cover pan and simmer 30 minutes.

3 Allow to cool slightly and liquidise until smooth. Add extra water or stock if too thick.

4 Return to pan and add the milk. Heat through gently. Do not allow to boil.

winter
warmers

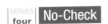

SERVES | **four** | **No-Check**

winter vegetable soup

- 3-4 medium carrots, diced
- 150g/5oz small white turnip, diced
- 1 large onion, chopped
- 3 sticks celery, finely sliced
- 2 Oxo vegetable cubes
- 900ml/1½ pints hot water
- Finely chopped parsley to garnish

1 Place vegetables in a large saucepan with 2 tbsp water. Bring to the boil, stir, cover and turn down heat. Leave vegetables to sweat gently 10 minutes.

2 Dissolve stock cubes in hot water and add to pan. Bring to the boil then lower heat, cover and simmer 10-15 minutes until vegetables are cooked.

3 Serve chunky, or crush with a potato masher and garnish with a little finely chopped parsley.

leek & 'neep' soup

SERVES **four** No-Check

300g/10 oz washed and sliced leeks
300g/10 oz white turnip, peeled and chopped
2 cloves garlic, chopped
900ml/1½ pints vegetable stock
black pepper

1 Place all the ingredients in a large saucepan. Bring to the boil, then lower heat, cover and simmer until vegetables are tender. Check and stir now and again.

2 Turn out heat and use a potato masher to crush vegetables. If too thick, add extra water.

3 Re-heat gently and serve sprinkled with black pepper.

variation...

Each serving may be sprinkled with 1 level dspn grated parmesan cheese. Add 20 calories, 1 Check, 2g fat

SERVES **four** 50 **2 0**

green velvet

- **400 g/14 oz frozen spinach**
- **300 ml/ ½ pint water**
- **2 Oxo vegetable cubes**
- **600 ml/1 pint skimmed milk**
- **2 tbsp lemon juice**

1 Put spinach, water and crumbled stock cubes into a saucepan and cook until spinach has defrosted and broken up.

2 Transfer to a blender. Liquidise, gradually adding the milk. Return to the saucepan, stir in the lemon juice and re-heat gently. Do not allow to boil.

3 If preparing in advance, do not add lemon juice until starting to re-heat.

variation...

Swirl 1 tbsp single cream into each bowl before serving. Add 25 calories, 1 Check, 2g fat.

or

Sprinkle each bowl with 1 dspn grated parmesan cheese before serving. Add 20 calories, 1 Check, 2g fat.

SERVES **four** | 50 **2** **0**

mushroom soup

350g/12 oz mushrooms, roughly chopped
1 large onion, finely chopped
400ml/14 fl.oz chicken or vegetable stock
600ml/1 pint skimmed milk
black pepper
freshly chopped parsley to garnish (optional)

1 Place mushrooms and onions in a large non-stick saucepan. Cover and cook over medium heat 5 minutes, stirring occasionally.

2 Remove lid and stir-fry 1-2 minutes more. Add stock and milk, bring to a simmer and cook 5 minutes, stirring frequently.

3 Allow to cool slightly, transfer to a blender and liquidise. Re-heat gently if necessary. Do not allow to boil.

4 Season with black pepper and serve garnished with a little freshly chopped parsley.

ham & pea soup

SERVES four | 100 **4** ②

- 600ml/1 pint vegetable stock
- 450g/1 lb frozen peas
- 1 small onion, finely chopped
- 115g/4oz potato, peeled and diced
- 60g/2oz lean smoked ham, finely chopped

1 Bring the stock to the boil in a large saucepan. Add the peas, onion and potato. Bring back to the boil, turn down heat, cover and simmer 20 minutes. Check and stir now and again.

2 Allow to cool slightly then liquidise until smooth.

3 Return soup to saucepan and stir in the ham. Bring to a simmer and heat through thoroughly, stirring almost continuously.

special
soup

SERVES	No-Check
3-4	

tomato & mint soup

3 medium onions, chopped
1 clove garlic, crushed
200 ml/$\frac{1}{3}$ pint chicken or vegetable stock
3 x 400g cans chopped tomatoes
6 tbsp freshly chopped mint
1 tbsp granulated sweetener

1 Place onions, garlic and stock into a large saucepan. Bring to the boil, turn down heat, cover and simmer 15 minutes, until soft. Remove lid and allow juices to reduce until thick and syrupy.

2 Add tomatoes and mint. Bring to the boil, turn down heat and simmer 15 minutes, uncovered.

3 Allow to cool slightly and stir in sweetener. Transfer to a blender and liquidise to a smooth purée.

4 Re-heat gently before serving.

SERVES	No-Check
6-8	

twin soup

To serve 6-8 people, make one quantity of Tomato & Mint Soup and one quantity of Celery & Celeriac Soup. To serve, transfer soups to two jugs and pour simultaneously from either side of the soup plate until they meet in the middle. Garnish with a small sprig of mint or celery leaf.

celery & celeraic soup

SERVES four | No-Check

1 medium head of celery, sliced
500g/18 oz celeriac, peeled and diced
2 medium onions, chopped
300 ml/½ pint chicken or vegetable stock
Additional stock may be required
black pepper

1 Place celery, celeriac, onions and stock in a large saucepan. Bring to the boil, cover tightly, reduce heat and simmer gently 20-30 minutes until vegetables are soft. Check and stir now and again.

2 Allow to cool slightly. Liquidise in two batches. Add some extra stock if necessary, but soup should be smooth and fairly thick.

3 Re-heat gently and serve sprinkled with black pepper.

| SERVES four | 90 | 4 | 6 |

straciatella

1200 ml/2 pints chicken stock, or make from 2 Knorr chicken stock cubes
4 tbsp dry or medium sherry
2 large eggs
4 dspn grated parmesan cheese
1 tsp finely chopped parsley

1 Put the stock and sherry into a saucepan and bring to the boil.

2 Beat the eggs lightly and stir in the parmesan cheese.

3 Turn down heat under saucepan to just below the boil and with a fork stir in the egg and cheese mixture. Continue to stir a few seconds as the eggs and cheese cook and form "threads".

4 Serve sprinkled with a little finely chopped parsley.

variation...

Can also be made with beef stock.

crab & sweetcorn soup

- **325g can sweetcorn kernels**
- **750ml/1¼ pints chicken stock**
- **2 spring onions, sliced**
- **1 dspn soy sauce**
- **2 tbsp dry sherry**
- **2 level tbsp cornflour**
- **85g/3oz fresh, canned or frozen white crabmeat**

1 Reserve quarter of the sweetcorn kernels and process the remaining corn and liquid in a blender until almost smooth.

2 Tip the sweetcorn into a saucepan together with the reserved kernels. Stir in the stock, spring onions and soy sauce. Bring to the boil, turn down heat, cover and simmer 10 minutes.

3 Mix the sherry with the cornflour. Pour into the soup, stirring continuously, and continue to stir and cook 1-2 minutes.

4 Stir in the crab meat and heat through a further 1-2 minutes.

SERVES four | 200 | 8 | 11

coconut, prawn & spring onion soup

2 spring onions, trimmed and sliced
2 level tbsp Thai red curry paste
400ml can reduced-fat coconut milk
600ml/1 pint chicken or fish stock
1 tsp light soy sauce or Thai fish sauce (nam pla)
200g/7oz cooked king prawns, defrosted if frozen
torn coriander or basil leaves to garnish

1 Place spring onions and curry paste into a large saucepan and stir-fry 1 minute. Shake can of coconut milk well before opening and pour into the pan stirring well.

2 Stir in the stock and soy sauce or Thai fish sauce and bring to just below the boil, stirring frequently. Turn down heat, add the king prawns and heat through gently, 1-2 minutes.

3 Serve soup garnished with a few torn coriander or small basil leaves.

salt sense

Stocks and stock cubes contain a lot of salt, but you can reduce the amount by diluting with more water. For example:

6g stock cube or 5g heaped tsp of stock granules should be plenty to make 300ml/½ pint stock rather than the 190-250ml often suggested.

11g stock cube can be used to make 600ml/1 pint stock rather than the 450ml often suggested.

Taste before adding any additional salt to soups, and if you must add, be very cautious and preferably use a reduced-sodium salt.